CHRISTIAN SCIENCE

BY
SALEM KIRBAN

Science and Health with Key to the Scriptures

DOCTRINES OF DEVILS
No. 4

Exposing the cults of our day

MOODY PRESS
CHICAGO

ACKNOWLEDGMENTS

To Dr. Gary G. Cohen, Professor of Greek and New Testament at Biblical School of Theology, Hatfield, Pennsylvania, who carefully checked the final manuscript and supplied the Scripture references for the fold-out chart.

To Bob Krauss, artist, who designed the fold-out chart.

To Doreen Frick, who typed the manuscript and skillfully proofread the book.

IT STARTED WITH A HORSE

It could be said with some degree of accuracy, that perhaps Mary Baker Eddy owes a portion of her gratitude to a horse.

Now this might initially seem unusual, and yet as we research the beginnings of Christianity being a science, we must start with the origins from which Mary Baker Eddy's basis of Christian Science began.

Phineas Parkhurst Quimby was born in Lebanon, New Hampshire, February 16, 1802. He eventually entered the practice of spiritual healing which won him a large reputation and led him to move to Portland, Maine in 1859. Quimby was very radical in opposing doctrinal conceptions of Christ. He uniformly called Jesus, "a man like ourselves," in order that he might win for the Master new recognition as the founder of spiritual science. To Quimby, "the Science of the Christ" was even greater than a religion.

Prior to Quimby's entering into the healing ministry in about 1833, he became very sick and was considered, as he stated, "fast wasting away with consumption."

In fact, he was so ill it was very difficult for him to walk, and he had taken so much calomel that he lost many of his teeth from the effect. Calomel is known today as mercurous chloride and was used chiefly in those days as a purgative. In those days "consumption" was a popular term among doctors, used to describe tuberculosis or any similar illness where there appeared to be a lack of energy. In fact, Quimby's illness seemed to have a scattering of everything according to his doctors, from diseased kidneys to lungs that were nearly wasted away, and to a liver that was also sick.

Because of this, he was compelled to abandon his business, and as he stated, "losing all hope, I gave up to die,—not that I thought the medical faculty had no wisdom, but that my case was one that could not be cured."

He goes on to state, "having an acquaintance who cured himself by riding horseback, I thought I would try riding in a carriage as I was too weak to ride horseback."

His horse, however, was not very cooperative. When he was about two miles from his home the horse suddenly decided to stop at the foot of a long hill and would not start up again. Quimby was obliged to get off the horse and to labor nearly the whole distance up the hill. Suddenly the horse started up again and passed Quimby.

It must have been an odd sight to see the horse galloping up the hill with Quimby trudging behind him. When Quimby finally reached the top of the hill, Quimby—not the horse—was exhausted. It was all he could do to get back in the carriage and sit. He was unable even at the top of the hill to get the horse to pull the carriage, and he thought he would have to sit in the carriage all day.

Finally, seeing a man ploughing, he asked him if he could start his horse. By this time, Quimby was so weak he could scarcely lift his whip to urge the horse to start. But suddenly, Quimby took possession of his faculties again, and drove the horse as fast as he could go up hill and down dale until he reached home. And when Quimby finally got the horse in the stable, a shocking discovery took place! He said that he suddenly realized that he felt as strong as he ever did before.

This experience with the horse was to be an indelible imprint on his mind, and was to be one of the factors in starting him on mesmerism—known today as hypnosis, and later into developing what is now known as mental healing or curing disease through the mind. Mr. Quimby became more and more convinced that disease was an error of the mind and not a real thing.

Later on we will cover Phineas P. Quimby's influence on Mary Baker Eddy, but it can be said with "tongue in cheek" that perhaps both Quimby and Mary Baker Eddy owe their start to a horse that wouldn't obey instructions.

ENTER MARY BAKER

Mary A. Morse Baker was born July 16, 1821 in the township of Bow, which is near the present city of Concord, New Hampshire. In those days the bicycle was still, for the most part, the fastest thing on the road. Life was hard and rugged in New England in winter. There was the struggle with the elements. And in the spring and summer the farmers had another struggle with the soil to try and eke out a meager existence.

There had been six generations of Bakers in New England before Mary Baker came on this pastoral scene. Her father, Mark Baker lived on his own farm of some 500 acres. Mark Baker was a Calvinist, and his fundamental beliefs in the Scripture were to cause conflict between him and his daughter who was to become the founder of Christian Science. Mrs. Eddy wrote in later years:

> My father's relentless theology emphasized belief in a final judgment day, in the danger of endless punishment, and in a Jehovah merciless towards unbelievers.[1]

Not much is known about Mark Baker's wife, Abigail, except that she was a very patient and a very industrious woman, and devoted all her energies to taking care of her family.

Mark Baker was very strict in his beliefs. He was active in the Congregational Church. He was always making sure that others in the congregation fulfilled their obligations to the church as he was fulfilling his. He brought charges of backsliding against fellow members when they failed to attend public worship or communion. In fact, the books of the Tilton Congregational Church record many a dispute between him and his fellow brethren.

All of the Baker children were born in a little farmhouse in Bow, between 1808 and 1821. There were three sons; Samuel, Albert, and George. There were also three daughters; Abigail, Martha, and Mary. Life ahead for him and his children was to be fraught with problems. In his later years, Mark Baker was afflicted with cancer. His two older daughters and their three children and two of his sons, Samuel and George all died deaths diagnosed as from cancer. We understand, therefore, with sympathy, why Mary was so concerned with science and health.

All the records appear to indicate that Mark Baker was both high-tempered and headstrong, and this trait was passed on to his children.

Of all the children born into the Baker household, Mary was the most sensitive. Perhaps this sensitivity to her own health also caused her to be concerned about the health of others—particularly

---

[1]Mary Baker Eddy, *Retrospection and Introspection* (Boston: The Christian Science Publishing Society, 1891), p. 13.

animals. She was always concerned whether the horses were too cold in the snow, or whether the hens were warm enough at night, or whether the ducks were distressed because the pond was frozen. Her grandmother tried to comfort her and assure her that God cared for all His creatures, but this assurance never seemed to satisfy Mary.

It was not unusual for her to arise several times at night in the cold winter, after she had been tucked into her warm bed, and go out to take care of the pigs in the farmyard. She could hear them squealing and she would become concerned and run down to the pen and sing to the pigs, because she felt they were lonely.

Irving C. Tomlinson in his book *Twelve Years with Mary Baker Eddy,* relates:

> It was natural for Mary to think of others before herself. In the fall she would go off into the woods with the other children after chestnuts and on returning home her father would say, 'Who pities father?' and Mary would instantly give him every nut she had gathered. 'You need not give away all you have, Mary,' cautioned her mother. 'You know the Bible says, 'Love thy neighbor as thyself.' It does not say 'Love thy neighbor better than thyself for justice belongs to both.'[2]

In Mark Baker's household it was important after the Sunday morning service for the children to sit still all day in the house with folded hands, listening to the reading of the Bible. This was more than Mary could stand, and Sundays became a day of torture for her. Perhaps some of this severe discipline led to her eventual hysterical attacks, and to her nervous condition which followed her through much of her life.

TIME OF DECISION

When Mary was twelve years old, her father Mark Baker decided it was time for her to make a formal profession of faith in their church. This disturbed Mary for she could not accept the doctrine of unconditional election, and endless punishment for those who did not accept Christ. She loved her brothers and sisters dearly and she knew that they had not yet made such a profession, and if her father's theology were correct it would mean that her brothers and sisters might be doomed to perpetual banishment from God. She refused to accept this.

---

[2]Irving C. Tomlinson, *Twelve Years with Mary Baker Eddy* (Boston: The Christian Science Publishing Society, 1945), p. 13.

Statue of Mary Baker Eddy at "Longyear" Museum in Brookline.

Nothing that Mark Baker said could change her mind. Mary stood her ground.

But in standing her ground, it affected her physically. She became so sick that Mark Baker had to race his horse to the nearest town to secure a doctor, shouting over and over again, "Mary is dying!"

However, Mary was not dying, but soon became well again. Looking back on this experience Mary Baker Eddy wrote:

> At the age of twelve I was admitted to the Congregational (Trinitarian) Church . . . the doctrine of unconditional election, or predestination, greatly troubled me: for I was unwilling to be saved, if my brothers and sisters were to be numbered among those who were doomed to perpetual banishment from God. So perturbed was I by the thoughts aroused by this erroneous doctrine, that the family doctor was summoned, and pronounced me stricken with fever . . .

> My mother, as she bathed my burning temples, bade me lean on God's love . . . The fever was gone . . . The physician marvelled; and the "horrible decree" of predestination . . . forever lost its power over me . . .

> I stoutly maintained [to the Church membership committee] that I was willing to trust God, and take my chance of spiritual safety with my brothers and sisters,—not one of whom had then made any profession of religion,—even if my creedal doubts left me outside the doors . . . .[3]

It was perhaps from this point onward that Mary Baker Eddy left the fundamentals of the faith to begin a new religion which she called Christian Science.

Mary's mother meant so much to her. Mary well recalled the time when her mother read to her from the Bible that Daniel prayed three times a day. What a deep impression this story made on her life. In fact, so much so that she actually prayed seven times a day in her childhood, and she would chalk down on the shed wall each prayer in succession. She even felt that she heard voices—the same as young Samuel.

It was Mary Morse Baker who had written to her girlfriend, Augusta Holmes:

> As to my being married I don't begin to think much of that decisive step, neither do I intend to be married at present. I am sure I feel as though I should like my liberty a little while longer.[4]

---

[3]Mary Baker Eddy, *Retrospection* . . ., pp. 13, 14.

[4]Hugh A. Studdert Kennedy, *Mrs. Eddy* (San Francisco: The Farallon Press, 1947), pp. 55, 56.

And in jest, she also wrote to Augusta suggesting that Augusta say something nice to a Mr. Dickey whom she apparently admired. She also suggested that she would enjoy the high responsibility of "making *cold*-hearted *man* raise his standard of female excellence, still higher."[5]

Perhaps Mary's first love was with her young friend, Andrew Gault, with whom she became acquainted while her family lived in Bow. When they moved to Sanbornton Bridge—the Tilton of today, this budding romance soon ceased, and she wrote this farewell verse:

> Hard is the task to take a final leave of
> friends of whom we shall see ah! never.
> With unaccustomed grief my bosom heaves
> And burns with latent fire forever.

A CHANCE MEETING LEADS TO MARRIAGE
GEORGE WASHINGTON GLOVER

A big wedding took place in 1832 when Mary was twelve years old. Her older brother, Samuel married Eliza Glover, daughter of John and Nancy Glover of Concord, New Hampshire.

Among those present at the wedding was the bride's young brother, George. It was at this ceremony that George and Mary became acquainted. Although Mary was only twelve and George Glover a little past eighteen, this initial experience was later to blossom into a marriage.

According to reports written at that time, Mary was a pretty girl, who usually let her hair hang in ringlets

Those who knew her said that Mary Baker's most striking beauty as a child lay in her big grey eyes, deep-set and overhung by dark lashes.

She loved pretty clothes and often made a ceremonious entrance into church, coming up the aisle after the rest of the congregation was seated and attracting the general attention of the audience. She even introduced to the little town of Bow, the "French twist," apparently a form of hair fashion, which in those days, was the last word.

---

[5]*Ibid.,* p. 55.

From early childhood until very late in Mrs. Eddy's life, she seemed to suffer attacks which resembled convulsions. Sometimes she would fall headlong to the floor, writhing and screaming in apparent agony. On another occasion, she dropped as if lifeless and lay limp until restored. At other times her muscles would become rigid and she would appear as though she lost contact with her environment. Perhaps this history of ill health had some additional bearing on her search for perfect peace and well-being.

When Mary Baker's brother, Samuel was married, Major George W. Glover, who was present at the wedding, took Mary on his knee and said he would return and make her his little wife. Mary at the time, being only twelve, ran from him and hid. Five years later, however, he came back to attend her sister Abigail's wedding. At that time he asked Mary to correspond with him, and through this correspondence they became further acquainted.

On December 12, 1843 a memorable event took place at Mark Baker's house in Bow. Mary Baker, 22, became the wife of George Washington Glover. A deep snow had covered the mountains and those who came to the wedding came in large sleighs.

The wedding ceremony was conducted by Dr. Enoch Corser, a special friend of Mary's and her teacher. When the wedding was over George and Mary bundled into a sleigh and took the road along the Winnepesaukee River towards Concord. This was their first stop in a long journey which was to end in Charleston, South Carolina. As they were leaving, Mary's mother, Abigail, handed George a little package. She had carefully sealed it, and asked that it not be opened until they were well on their journey.

It was not unusual for Abigail Baker, Mary's mother, to give a special gift to her daughter and new son-in-law. Every mother is torn between tears and smiles when they see a daughter, whom they love, leave the old homestead for marriage and for what will prove to be a most complex experience.

The honeymoon journey by ship was very rough, and Mary became seasick. But as they sailed south the storm soon passed, and together Mary and George opened the package that Abigail Baker had given them. There was no letter inside, but just a little book of poems by Lydia Sigourney. One of the poems was marked. It is most certain that this poem conveyed to George all that Mary's mother wanted to tell him.

Deal gently, thou, when, far away,
'Mid stranger scenes her feet shall rove,
Nor let thy tender cares decay—
The soul of woman lives on love;
And should'st thou, wondering, mark a tear
Unconscious from her eyelid break,
Be pitiful, and soothe the fear
That man's strong heart can ne'er partake.
A mother yields her gem to thee,
On the true breast to sparkle rare—
She places 'neath thy household tree
The idol of her fondest care;
And by trust to be forgiven,
When judgment wakes in terror wild,
By all thy treasured hopes of heaven,
Deal gently with my darling child.

FROM JOY TO TRAGEDY

George Glover had built a fairly prosperous business in Charleston, South Carolina.

And in February 1844, Mary accompanied her husband on a business trip to Wilmington, North Carolina.

However, just six months after he was married, George Washington Glover was stricken with yellow fever, and died in June 1844 at Wilmington. By August, Mary Baker Glover was back in Sanbornton and her romance was at an end.

But Mary Baker Glover was going to have a baby, and her son was born on September 12, 1844. He was named for his father, George Washington Glover II.

Apparently childbirth affected her, and it became necessary for Mahala Sanborn, a blacksmith's daughter, to become her faithful nurse. In fact, even her father, Mark Baker, had to for hours hold his nerve-wracked daughter in his arms, and rock her gently to and fro. He would enforce strict silence in the house, and even took the precaution to deaden the clatter made by passers-by by placing straw and tan bark on the road outside.

The slightest noise affected her, and for all practical purposes her son was brought up by other interested friends, until he reached his adult years. So intense was Mary's desire for swinging that not only was she rocked to sleep like a child in the arms of her father, but a large cradle was made for her so that she could fall asleep.

Sometimes when things got desperate, Mark Baker would send for old "Boston John" Clark to come and quiet Mrs. Glover by hypnotism. When Mary's mother, Abigail, died of typhoid fever in November, 1849, this was a real blow to her, for she and her mother had been very close. Soon it became almost impossible for her to care for her child. Her father, Mark Baker, married again, and her old home took on a new atmosphere. At any rate, Mary's son George, was reared by Mahala Sanborn who then married Russell Cheney, and upon their marriage, little George Glover was taken to their new home in North Groton. For some time Mary's son was called by the Cheney name.

In a later book called *Retrospection and Introspection,* Mary states:

> After his removal, a letter was read to my little son, informing him that his mother was dead and buried. Without my knowledge a guardian was appointed him, and I was then informed that my son was lost.[6]

Mary was never to see her son again until he reached the age of 34, had a wife and two children. With the death of her mother and the loss of her son, Mary was desolate, and she knew of no one to whom she could turn.

MARRIAGE NO. 2
DANIEL PATTERSON

Apparently she never lacked admirers, however, and one of her suitors at that time was Dr. Daniel Patterson. Dr. Patterson was a tall man, with a full flowing black beard, very well-dressed, wearing "varnished boots," a Prince Albert coat, and a silk top hat. He was an itinerant dentist, practicing in Tilton and in other villages in the area.

The wedding took place June 21, 1853 at Mark Baker's house. However, Mary was so ill that Dr. Patterson had to carry his bride downstairs from her room for the ceremony and then carry her back up again when it was all over.

In fact, she sent for her cradle again, and it was necessary for Dr. Patterson to bring a large wagon containing his wife's cradle back into Tilton. From Tilton they moved to North Groton, and because of her nervous condition she required her husband to keep the wooden bridge over the brook covered with sawdust to deaden the sound of footsteps or vehicles.

Mrs. Glover wrote that her dominant thought in marrying Dr. Pat-

[6]Mary Baker Eddy, *Retrospection* . . . ., p. 21.

terson was to get back her child. But after her marriage, Dr. Patterson was not willing that her son, George Glover, should have a home with them.

This son of Mary, George Glover, in later years made an excellent record as a soldier in the Civil War, and later became a United States Marshall in the Dakotas, and finally settled in Lead, South Dakota, where he carried on a mining enterprise. He had a wife and four children, but none of them ever became Christian Scientists.

Dr. Patterson, Mary's second husband, however, was apparently a gracious man, who was popular among his patrons, although he apparently was not a genius at making money. He waited upon Mary constantly, carrying her downstairs to her meals and back again to her room.

However, the marriage was said not to have been a very happy one, with Dr. Patterson's rather coarse geniality, and Mary's high-strung nervous condition. It was probably a relief to both of them when Dr. Patterson went South after the Civil War in the hopes of securing more profitable employment as an Army surgeon.

He was caught behind the enemy lines and was taken captive and sent to a Southern prison. One day upon returning home after escaping back into Union lines, Dr. Patterson eloped with one of his patients and Mary was granted a divorce. It is said that Dr. Patterson gave his wife an annuity of $200 annually for several years after their separation.

After roving from town to town, Dr. Patterson finally ended up at his boyhood home at Saco, Maine, where he lived the life of a hermit until his death in 1896.

The years from 1844 to 1866 could be considered the blank years of Mary Baker Eddy's life. These 22 lost years between her 23rd and 46th birthdays were spent in ill health and discontent.

ENTER QUIMBY

While Dr. and Mrs. Patterson were still married, they heard of a new healer, Phineas Parkhurst Quimby of Portland, Maine who would soon visit the Concord, New Hampshire area to treat those who were sick.

Quimby's initial occupation was as a clockmaker. In fact "Quimby clocks" can still be found in some parts of Maine. However, in the 1830's, influenced by a French hypnotist, Charles Poyen,

Quimby became interested in healing.

Dr. Patterson wrote to Dr. Quimby on October 14, 1861 and told him that Mrs. Patterson (Mary) had been an invalid from a spinal disease for many years. Nothing came of this letter.

However, the following spring, Mrs. Patterson herself wrote to Quimby appealing for him to help her. Finally in October, 1862, Mary Patterson was able to see Dr. Quimby in his office at the International Hotel in Portland, Maine.

Although he was known as Dr. Quimby, he was not a "doctor." He had no university degree and had studied in no regular school of medicine. He gave no drugs, yet he professed to make his patients well and happy, purely by the benevolent power of the mind.

Upon visiting Dr. Quimby, Mary wrote in the Portland *Evening Courier:*

> In less than one week from that time [I first visited P.P. Quimby] I ascended by a stairway of 182 steps to the dome of the city hall and am improving ad infinitum.

Quimby himself had no love for doctors. He stated:

> Instead of gaining confidence in the doctors, I was forced to the conclusion that their science is false. Man is made up of truth and belief; and, if he is deceived into a belief that he has, or is liable to have, a disease, the belief is catching, and the effect follows it.[7]

Quimby went on to state:

> They make ten diseases to one cure, thus bringing a surplus of misery into the world, and shutting out a healthy state of society. They have a monopoly, and no theory that lessens disease can compete with them. . . .My theory teaches man to manufacture health.[8]

He also went on to write:

> Eternal life is Christ, or Science. Science rises above all narrow ideas. He who is scientific in regard to health and happiness is his own law, and not subject to the laws of man, except as he is deceived or ignorant. . . .The Science that I try to practice is the Science that was taught 1800 years ago and has never had a place in the heart of man since, but is in the world, and the world knows it not.[9]

---

[7]Horatio W. Dresser, *The Quimby Manuscripts,* (New York: Thomas Y. Crowell Company, 1921), p. 29.

[8]*Ibid.,* p. 29.

[9]*Ibid.,* pp. 137-38, 144.

"Longyear," home of Mary Baker Eddy Museum, Brookline, Massachusetts.

Mary was a prolific letter writer and her many letters to Dr. Phineas P. Quimby attest to her gratitude for his ability to relieve her of her many illnesses. In a letter written January 12, 1863 from Sanbornton Bridge, she wrote to Dr. Quimby, in part:

> Your angel visit here removed all my stomach pains, the particulars of which were very remarkable. . .I am to all who once knew me a living wonder, and a living monument of your power. . . .

What Mary described as an angel visit was the belief that Dr. Quimby could heal even though not physically present with the individual who was ill.

In an article written in 1861, Quimby stated:

> My arguments are based upon my knowledge of his (the patient's) feelings, and this knowledge put in practice is the Science of Health, and is for the benefit of the sick. . . .[10]

He went on to say:

> Every disease is the invention of man and has no identity and Wisdom. . . .[11]

One of Quimby's most revealing statements was made about 1865 when he wrote:

> Within the last seven years I have sat with more than twelve thousand different persons. . .therefore I know what I say is true: that if there had never been a physician in the world there would not have been $\frac{1}{10}$ of the suffering. It is also true that religious creeds have made a very large class of persons miserable, but religion like all creeds based on superstition must give way to Science.[12]

It was this background of teaching that filled the mind of Mary Baker Eddy, and it was to have an influence on her in her later years. When she wrote in the Portland *Evening Courier* in 1862 of the recovery she had from her illness, through the healing hand of Dr. P. P. Quimby, she answered a criticism of that article by stating:

> P. P. Quimby rolls away the stone from the sepulchre of error, and health is the resurrection.

Undoubtedly these many letters written by Mary Baker Eddy in

---

[10]*Ibid.,* pp. 248-49.

[11]*Ibid.,* p. 269.

[12]*Ibid.,* pp. 276-77.

her early years, attesting her gratitude to Dr. Quimby for this new Science of health and healing, are a source of embarrassment to the Christian Science Church today, which has constantly sought to disown Quimby, and to place Mary Baker Eddy as the founder of Christian Science.

In a sense, however, she actually was the founder of Christian Science. She gave it impetus and direction, using Quimby's early instruction only as a beginning point from which was to rise a cult with far greater influence and far greater dimension.

Quimby treated all who came to him, whether they could pay or not, and often times he didn't accept money. "People," he would say, "send for me and the undertaker at the same time; and the one who gets there first gets the case."

Quimby was convinced that he had solved the riddle of life and that in the end the whole world would accept his ideas. Quimby was a copious writer. In six years he produced ten volumes of manuscripts—although most of his writings were never published. All during her stay in Portland, Mary Patterson was almost constantly in Dr. Quimby's office asking him questions, reading his manuscripts, and observing his treatment of his patients.

Perhaps, Dr. Quimby saw in Mrs. Patterson a woman who could assist him in popularizing his doctrines and putting them into a published form.

In another letter written from Saco, Maine, September 14, 1863, Mrs. Patterson stated that Quimby's "angel visits" (absent treatments) were helping her. She wrote, "I would like to have you in your omnipresence visit me at eight o'clock this evening." She further went on to state that she wished to be treated for "small beliefs," namely, "stomach trouble and backache."

Phineas Parkhurst Quimby died January 16, 1866. He had for years suffered from an abdominal tumor. He had never had it treated by a doctor, and evidently, was not able to heal himself.

Perhaps no one felt greater grief over Quimby's death than Mary M. Patterson.

IT BEGAN WITH AN ICY SIDEWALK

Much of Christian Science tradition places great emphasis on Mary's healing in Lynn, Massachusetts.

She fell on the icy sidewalk near the corner of Market and Oxford

Streets in Swampscott (a suburb of Lynn), and injured her back. She stated that she:

> . . .came to consciousness amid a storm of vapours from cologne, chloroform, ether, camphor, etc.
>
> But to find myself the helpless cripple I was before I saw Dr. Quimby. The physician attending said I had taken the last step I ever should, but in two days I got out of my bed *alone* and *will* walk. . . .[13]

She stated in later years that after reading the account of Jesus healing the man sick of the palsy, she was able to cure herself, and ever after was in better health than she had previously enjoyed.

Actually, Mary Baker Eddy dated her discovery of Christian Science as beginning from this experience in Lynn, Massachusetts.

The earliest names Mrs. Eddy called her teachings were Moral Science, Christian Healing, Mental Healing and Christian Science Mind Healing.

> In the year 1866, I discovered the Science of Metaphysical Healing, and named it Christian Science. God had been graciously fitting me, during many years, for the reception of a final revelation of the absolute Principle of Scientific Mind-healing. . . .No human pen or tongue taught me the Science contained in this book. . .and neither tongue nor pen can overthrow it.[14]

This quotation was printed from the 1898 edition of *Science and Health,* pages 1 and 4.

After her husband, Daniel Patterson deserted her in 1866, Mary's sister, Abigail, offered to build Mary a house right next door to her own, so that Mary could pursue her writing undisturbed.

There was only one condition—that she give up her "queer ideas" and return to the church of which Abigail was a member.

Mary did not accept the offer. Shortly thereafter she left Lynn, Massachusetts, to join her friends in Christian Science, the Crafts, at Stoughton.

In many of her writings after that she consistently played down any

---

[13]Georgine Milmine, *The Life of Mary Baker G. Eddy,* (New York: *McClure's Magazine,* 1907), volume 28, p. 510.

[14]Mary Baker Eddy, *Science and Health,* (Boston: The Christian Science Publishing Society, 1898), pp. 1, 4.

affect that Phineas Quimby had on her new religion, and in fact stated:

> No works on the subject of Christian Science existed, prior to my discovery of this Science. Before the publication of my first work on this doctrine, a few manuscripts of mine were in circulation. The discovery and founding of Christian Science has cost more than thirty years of unremitting toil and unrest. . .
>
> In the latter half of the nineteenth century I discovered the Science of Christianity. . .
>
> In 1895 I ordained that the Bible, and *Science and Health with Key to the Scriptures*, the Christian Science textbook, be the pastor, on this planet, of all the churches of the Christian Science denomination. . .
>
> Whenever and wherever a church of Christian Science is established, its pastor is the Bible and my book.[15]

In June of 1887 she was to write in the *Christian Science Journal:*

> As long ago as 1844 I was convinced that mortal mind produced all disease, and that the various medical systems were, in no proper sense, scientific.

Apparently through her theories of progressive revelation, she claims to have discovered the principles of mental healing on three different dates, which include:

1853 (in a letter to the *Boston Post* of March 7, 1883)
1864 (in the first edition of *Science and Health* of 1875)
1866 (from *Retrospection and Introspection*)

In her own words, however, in the *Christian Science Journal* of June 1887, she commented that before her visit to Quimby in 1862, "I knew nothing of the Science of Mind-healing . . . . Mind Science was unknown to me."

Christian Science makes much of Mary Baker Eddy's fall on the sidewalk on February 3, 1866, and it is at this point they believe Christian Science actually began. At that time she claimed that a Dr. Cushing pronounced her injury incurable and stated that she could not survive three days because of it.

However, Dr. Cushing who was living in Springfield, Massachusetts and was the president of the Massachusetts Homeopathic Society,

---

[15]Mary Baker Eddy, *Miscellaneous Writings*, (Boston. The Christian Science Publishing Society, 1896), pp. 382,383.

stated in an affidavit that:

> I did not at any time declare, or believe, that there was no hope for Mrs. Patterson's recovery, or that she was in a critical condition, and did not at any time say, or believe, that she had but three or any other limited number of days to live.[16]

Mrs. Eddy claimed that she named her discovery Christian Science in 1866.

However, there are manuscripts which show that Phineas Parkhurst Quimby called his theory Christian Science as early as 1863.

FROM HOME TO HOME

In the years to follow, Mary Patterson Eddy was to be shuffled from one home to another. Because of her intense desire to promote her new theology and because of her nervous personality, she was not the easiest person to get along with. Soon after being invited in a home to stay, she would outwear her welcome and be asked to leave.

When she refused her sister Abigail's offer of a home, she traveled over a hundred miles by stagecoach and train from Sanbornton to Taunton to stay at the home of Hiram Crafts.

As Irving C. Tomlinson says in *Twelve Years with Mary Baker Eddy*, this was to begin:

> . . . the consecrated labor of years; years of unending effort and constant study, of poverty and privation, of scorn and ridicule, of misunderstanding, suspicion, desertion, and betrayal.[17]

Mary joined the Crafts in the early part of 1867, and for some months lived in their home at East Stoughton . . . which is now Avon. Mary Crafts' brother, Ira Holmes, later related that Mary's husband Hiram S. Crafts had entered into an agreement with Mrs. Patterson to pay her a certain sum of money for instructing him in "Quimby's Science."

Hiram Crafts was the first student of Mrs. Eddy's to go into practice, and he placed an ad in the Taunton newspaper May 13, 1867. It was at this time that Mr. Crafts had moved from East Stoughton to Taunton, taking with him his wife and Mrs. Eddy.

Apparently Mrs. Eddy's all-absorbing teaching was monopolizing too much of Mr. Crafts' time—much to the consternation of Mary Crafts.

---

[16]In an affidavit, January 2, 1907, in Springfield, Massachusetts. Sworn before Raymond A. Bidwell, *Notary Public*.

[17]Tomlinson, *Twelve Years. . .*, p. 38.

The exact details of this dispute may never be known. Ira Holmes in a sworn statement of February 7, 1907 stated that Mrs. Patterson urged Mr. Crafts to get a bill of divorce from his wife, Mary Crafts. Holmes, in part, said:

> The reason Mrs. Patterson gave for urging Mr. Crafts to divorce his wife was, that Mrs. Crafts stood in the way of the success of Mr. Crafts and Mrs. Patterson in the healing business.

Mr. Crafts decided that he could get along without Mrs. Patterson, and this began one of many sudden departures from households for Mary Baker Patterson Eddy.

Her next "haven in the storm" took her to Amesbury, a little town in Massachusetts near the New Hampshire border. Here, through recommendation from a friend, she was welcomed by the Websters. It was here that she was to meet an energetic 18 year old lad, by the name of Richard Kennedy, who was self-employed in making boxes, but who one day would figure prominently in Christian Science.

Mrs. Mary Baker Patterson's stay here was not very long either. When Mrs. Webster's son-in-law, William Ellis came up from New York, he commanded Mary to leave. When she refused to do so, he had her trunk dragged from her room and set outside the door, and insisted upon her also going out the door. When she was outside, he closed the door and locked it. It was dark at the time, and a heavy rain was falling.

It was experiences like this that probably caused Mary Baker Eddy to write a poem in 1867 titled, "Alone."

> I've sought the home my childhood gave—
> A moment's shelter from the wave
> Then those when sick, whose pain I bore,
> A Sister drove me from the door.
> O weary heart, O tired sigh,
> So wronged to live—alone I'd die.

It must have been a pathetic scene to see Mary packing her few belongings, and moving on at repeated short intervals, carrying with her a pile of papers tied up with a string, which had grown bulkier and bulkier.

The more it grew, the more she treasured it.

She called it her Bible. And it was from these papers the now world-wide Christian Science movement would some day emerge.

chilDREN CAN'T hElp WONDERING.

And they wonder a lot about God. They seem to have a natural awareness that He's here, and that He's important. But they want to know more. In the Christian Science Sunday School, God's nearness and goodness become practical realities to children. They study and discuss weekly Bible Lessons, and how to apply their truths each day. They learn to look to God for His unfailing help.

No need for your child to go on wondering. Let him start discovering, at our Sunday School. We'll be delighted to welcome him and his friends.

CHRISTIAN SCIENCE SUNDAY SCHOOL

10:30 AM

FIRST CHURCH OF CHRIST, SCIENTIST

515 North Main Street

Prayer heals

Proof that prayer does heal is given every Wednesday at all Christian Science churches during testimonial meetings. Hear how harmony and healing have come into the life of your neighbor. Why not accept this invitation to learn how prayer heals as understood and applied in Christian Science.

Christian Science Testimonial Meetings

Every Wednesday

For the time and location of the church nearest you in the following counties, call:

LOS ANGELES (213) 776-0517   RIVERSIDE (714) 684-3958
ORANGE (714) 535-4818   SAN BERNARDINO (714) 885-1870

Newspaper ads run by Christian Science churches.

Perhaps Hugh A. Studdert Kennedy's explanation of the difference between the Quimby method and the Mary Baker Eddy method is the most concise:

> Quimby declared that mind was stronger than matter, and that, through certain strange and devious methods, this could be practically demonstrated.
>
> Mary Baker Eddy in her manuscript declared that "Mind can overcome matter and all materiality in the human consciousness, *not* because Mind is stronger than matter and all materiality, but because Mind is the only reality, and matter and all materiality are in the realms of illusion."[18]

THE $300 FEE

Richard Kennedy soon left the box business and became a devoted student of Mary's. It was not too long before Mary Patterson and Richard Kennedy moved into an office in Lynn, Massachusetts, in the summer of 1870. Outside the front door was a sign which simply read, "Dr. Kennedy."

From the very beginning he was extraordinarily successful . . . primarily because he was able to heal the sick.

Many of Kennedy's patients wanted to know more about this new theory called Christian Science, and this is where Mary Patterson took up the work. At first, she talked to each one individually. She had been doing this type of teaching for a number of years, but she soon realized that individualized teaching would be impractical if she were to build her long dreamed of work. Her greatest problem was what type of fee to charge for her teaching. She was very astute in realizing that the human mind never values highly what it secures easily and cheaply.

It must be remembered that at this time the average wage was less than $1,000 a year. Yet, the amazing thing was that Mary Patterson decided on a fee of $300 for a course of twelve lessons. This fee was never changed. In those days, this amounted to about one third of the annual income of an individual!

Can you imagine if Mary Baker Eddy's program were in effect today? These twelve lessons would cost some $3500 to $4000!

And another amazing item is that each of the twelve lessons was only about a one-half hour talk!

Can you imagine paying $4000 for six hours of lecture?

---

[18]Kennedy, *Mrs. Eddy. . . ,* p. 163.

This will give you some idea of what her students gladly paid in the 1870's to learn of her new Science of Health.

These twelve lessons covered a period of three weeks, and in some cases she did receive students without charge, but in the final settlement always gave them a receipt in full for $300 . . . even those who did not pay.

Already in those days she saw the possibilities of what her new-found theories could blossom into.

She more than once told her associate, Kennedy, that one day she would establish a great religion that would reverence her as its founder and source. "Richard," she would declare, "you will live to hear the church bells ring out my birthday."

And this prediction by her did come true on July 16, 1904, when the church bells rang her birthday at Concord, New Hampshire.

At this time, Mary Baker had professional cards printed up which simply stated

---

MARY M. GLOVER
Teacher of
Moral Science

In 1888, Mrs. Eddy reduced the course of twelve lessons to seven. However, the tuition fee still remained at $300. There are conflicting stories on the sudden separation of Richard Kennedy from the Christian Science movement. The 1906 and 1907 issues of *McClure's Magazine* tell the story. Here, in the writings of Georgine Milmine, the wife of a newspaper man in Rochester, New York, we read:

> The split between Kennedy and Mrs. Glover occurred over a dispute in a card game played on Thanksgiving night of 1871, when Mrs. Glover accused Kennedy of cheating in the game of cards.

However official Christian Science publications state that Mary Baker Eddy was disturbed by Richard Kennedy's use of manipulation in his healing methods. It was stated that his treatment consisted of manipulation of the head and solar plexus. The solar plexus is an area situated in the upper part of the abdomen which contains a network of nerves located behind the stomach, and in the front of the aorta. Richard Kennedy found this treatment especially effective in treating women as Hugh A. Studdert Kennedy states in his book, *Mrs. Eddy*:

> The very ceremony of taking down the hair before 'treatment,' and drying and putting it up again afterwards, suggested to them that something important was being done in their behalf, and they responded most favorably.[19]

Mrs. Eddy was later to write in her first edition of *Science and Health* which was published a few years later,

> Sooner suffer a doctor infected with smallpox to be about you than come under the treatment of one that manipulates his patients' heads and is a traitor to science.[20]

After the partnership split, Mrs. Patterson's share of the receipts was some $6,000.

Many storms of dissent were to follow in Mrs. Eddy's wake. One dissatisfied student, Wallace W. Wright, demanded that Mrs. Eddy not only return his tuition but also $200 extra in damages. He, however, promised that if Mrs. Patterson could give a public demonstration of the practical value of her teaching, he would retract all his charges.

Among the methods of proof he wanted Mrs. Eddy to use were:

1. to restore the dead to life again;
2. to walk upon the water without the aid of artificial means;
3. to live 24 hours without air;
4. to restore sight when the optic nerve had been destroyed;
5. to set and heal a broken bone without the aid of artificial means.

Mary Patterson ignored this challenge.

REFLECTIONS AT RED ROCK

From her bitter experience with Richard Kennedy, Mary Patterson was convinced that her teaching would never be safe from misrepresentation until she had transferred it from written manuscript form into a printed book. Many times from the summer of 1872 until about 1876 she could be seen in the afternoon making her way along the cowpaths at the red rocks at Lynn, carrying a book and a roll of papers. For her, the writing of her first book called, *Science and Health,* was a tremendous physical task. There were some 150,000 words in this first edition, and all of this had to be written in long-hand.

---

[19]Kennedy, *Mrs. Eddy. . . ,* p. 174.

[20]Mary Baker Eddy, *Science and Health,* first edition . . . , p. 193.

Mary at this time was rooming with Mr. and Mrs. George Clark. George Clark had just finished a book of his own, *A Boy's Story of Seagoing Life*. So George and Mary together went to see a book publisher in Boston on the possibility of publishing George's book as well as the prospects for Mary's coming volume on Christian Science.

George's book was accepted at once. Mary's was rejected equally as fast. As they were returning home, Mary suddenly took hold of George's arm as they passed the church, and said quietly, "I shall have a church of my own someday."[21]

This statement was one day to become a reality.

Yet time and time again she was to suffer the pangs of loneliness, and on Thanksgiving Day she wrote a letter to a friend stating in part:

> They tell me this day is set apart for festivities and rejoicing, but I have no evidence of this . . . . I am alone today . . . . Family ties are broken, never to be reunited in this world with me . . . .

THE FIRST HEADQUARTERS

In March of 1875, Mary M. B. Glover purchased a property at Number Eight Broad Street in Lynn, Massachusetts. This small two and a half story building was surrounded by a narrow strip of lawn and it had a shade tree in one corner. She retained a large classroom on the ground floor and a little attic on the third floor lighted by a sky light in the roof, that could be pushed upwards to secure ventilation. Here she completed her manuscript. On the wall was a framed text from the Bible, which said, "Thou shalt have no other Gods before Me."

Mary was home at last. The vacant rooms were quickly filled by those eager to become students under her teaching. This became the first official headquarters of Christian Science. Her next important student who was to do well was Daniel Harrison Spofford. In less than a month after he entered her class, he opened up an office in Lynn, putting out the sign:

DR. SPOFFORD
Scientific Physician

On Sunday, June 6, in 1875, the first public Christian Science meeting was held in the Templar's Hall at Lynn. There were about 60 people there, and Mrs. Patterson was paid $5.00 each

---

[21]Kennedy, *Mrs. Eddy* . . . p. 188.

week to bring the message. These regular meetings were short-lived however, and after the fifth meeting the public Sunday services were abandoned.

A DREAM FULFILLED

Mary Baker Eddy was determined that her book would be published, but no publisher could be found who would even consider the book. It was then that two friends, George Barry and Elizabeth Newhall finally decided to advance the money and publish the book themselves. They named themselves, "The Christian Science Publishing Company."

In the fall of 1875, the Christian Science Publishing Company had completed the great task. Mary Baker Eddy's dream was beginning to be fulfilled.

The book was published under the title, *Science and Health*. One thousand copies were printed, and it was sold for $2.50 a copy. Daniel Spofford was placed in charge of sales.

Hugh A. Studdert Kennedy, in his book, *Mrs. Eddy*, quotes:

> Between the appearance of the first edition in 1875, and the last in 1908, *Science and Health* ran through 382 editions. And in many of these, changes of considerable importance were made, especially in the early editions. In the sixteenth edition issued in 1885, the book was completely rearranged and to a large extent rewritten, and yet the author never read it through consecutively until it had been out more than thirty years.[22]

Mrs. Eddy believed that Christian Science differed from orthodox Christianity in nothing except that it was, "a step more spiritual."[23]

MARRIAGE NO. 3
ASA GILBERT EDDY

In those days there was no such thing as Women's Liberation Movements, or equal rights for women, and for Mary Baker Glover Patterson to emerge as a leader of a religious movement was a constant struggle.

There were many times when people whom she trusted failed her. How she longed to spend as much time as possible in writing her new

[22]Kennedy, *Mrs. Eddy* . . ., p. 204.

[23]Mary Baker Eddy, *The People's Idea of God*. Sermon, *Prose Works*, (Boston: The Christian Science Publishing Society, 1886). p. 1

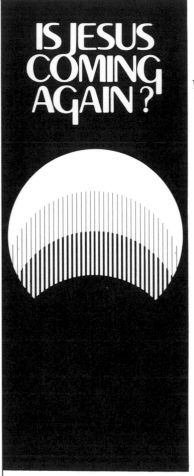

IS JESUS COMING AGAIN?

What does Christian Science have to say about the second coming?

To understand the Christian Scientist's viewpoint, it is necessary first to understand the definitions he accepts for *Jesus* and *Christ*.

Thus Christian Science makes a significant distinction between Jesus and the Christ he came to reveal. Jesus was a man, a human being, born of Mary. The Christ is the divine message— the truth of being—Jesus brought to mankind.

As you begin to study Christian Science, you soon realize that the corporeal Jesus is not coming back to earth.

Mrs. Eddy writes, "The second appearing of Jesus is, unquestionably, the spiritual advent of the advancing idea of God, as in Christian Science."[7]

A current Christian Science leaflet on the Second Coming with excerpts of its contents.

theology, and often students and friends would impose on her time. The situation grew acute.

To one in whom she had placed confidence, and who was not living up to her expectations, she wrote:

> Now, Dr. Spofford, won't you exercise *reason*, and let me live or will you *kill* me? Your mind is just what has brought on my relapse, and I shall never *recover* if you do not govern yourself and TURN YOUR THOUGHTS wholly away from me . . . won't you *quit thinking* of me.
> I shall write no more to a male student and never more trust one to live with . . . I shall never again trust a man . . . .[24]

She believed that in unburdening the souls of others, that these same trials or illnesses were in effect transferred to her shoulders.

Soon someone was to come on the scene that was to change her life, and his name was to become associated with Christian Science and made famous throughout the world.

His name, Asa Gilbert Eddy.

On January 12, 1877, Mary wrote to a friend:

> Last Spring Dr. Eddy came to me a hopeless invalid. I saw him then for the first time, and but twice. When his health was so improved he next came to join my class (his residence was South Boston). In four weeks after he came to study he was in practice doing well, worked up an excellent reputation for healing and at length won my affections on the ground alone of his great goodness and strength of character.

Asa had a very unusual mother, Betsey Smith Eddy. Although brought up in the mountains of Vermont as a farmer, Asa's mother was not a very good housekeeper and she had a passion for driving.

After seeing her children to school she would often set out with her horse and buggy and drive for the entire day around the countryside. In fact, to protect herself from rough weather, she devised an ingenious costume.

It looked like a helmet that a diver would wear for deep-sea diving.

On the front of her large bonnet she hung a shawl. In the shawl she inserted a 9 x 10 pane of window glass. This window glass was so placed that when she donned the costume the glass was opposite her face. The children of the village called her, "The woman with the looking glass."

Asa's family had no church connections. So whenever one of her children was sick, she would call in "Sleeping Lucy."

---

[24]Kennedy, *Mrs. Eddy* . . ., p. 220.

"Sleeping Lucy" would come to the house and pass into a sleep or deep trance, and in this state, she supposedly was able to diagnose cases of sickness and to prescribe remedies for them.

When Asa Gilbert Eddy left home about 1860, he first went to Springfield, Vermont to work in a woolen mill, and then finally in a baby carriage factory. He was able to save enough money to buy the family farm from his parents and then acted as a sewing machine agent. It was here that he became acquainted with Daniel H. Spofford—going to him as a patient. Eventually enrolling in Mrs. Patterson's class, he became acquainted with Mary Baker Glover Patterson.

They were married on New Year's Day 1877. They received many unusual gifts on their wedding day. One was a cake basket made of silver. Another was a bouquet of crystallized geranium leaves of rare varieties encased in glass.

Gilbert was a very methodical man, and it was stated, "He could do up a shirt as well as any woman." In fact, even at the wedding he was moving about quietly, tidying up the room, putting chairs back in their places, stacking up the plates, carrying them to the pantry, and putting the remains of the wedding cake back in the cake box.

When Asa Eddy showed the marriage license to Dr. Spofford, Dr. Spofford noticed that the ages of both the bride and groom were put down as forty years. Dr. Spofford was aware that Mary Glover Patterson was actually fifty-six years old. He remarked upon this inaccuracy. Mr. Eddy explained that the statement of age was a mere formality.

There are several instances in those years of attempted plagiarism of Mrs. Eddy's *Science and Health,* and so one of Asa Gilbert Eddy's first assignments was to go to Washington to make an exhaustive study of the copyright laws in the Library of Congress. Mrs. Eddy accompanied her husband and they spent three months there studying the law.

It is interesting to note that Congress passed an unusual law recently. President Nixon signed a bill in December of 1971, giving Christian Scientists a 75-year extension of their copyright on the basic text of their faith.

Exclusive monopoly rights to the 1906 work—*Science and Health With Key to the Scriptures* by the late Mary Baker Eddy—were assigned to Mrs. Eddy's trustees in the movement giving them control over past and future editions and preventing publication by other sources.

Christian Scientist leaders wanted the copyright to preserve the purity of the text and to permit congregations throughout the movement to follow its exact page numbers.

Sen. Jacob K. Javits (R., N.Y.), backed by the New York State Bar Association, opposed the bill, arguing that the restriction would prevent dissident groups in the movement from publishing their own versions of the text. Javits said it was a protection that had never in history been given either to a religious or nonreligious writing.

Shortly after their return from Washington to Boston, Asa Eddy became ill.

As he grew steadily worse, Mrs. Eddy finally sent for a regular physician who identified Eddy's illness as a disease of the heart, which could kill him at any moment.

On June 3, 1882, Asa Gilbert Eddy died.

Although she had previously stated that she did not believe in postmortem examinations of patients, she telegraphed Dr. Noyes to come up from Lynn and perform an autopsy on her husband. She maintained that her husband had died from mental arsenic.

To dispute this, Dr. Noyes actually took Mr. Eddy's heart into the room where she was and pointed out for her its defects—according to a statement by newspaper reporter Georgine Milmine.

However, on the following Monday, June 5, 1882, she issued a statement to the *Boston Post* stating:

> My husband's death was caused by malicious mesmerism . . .
> I know it was poison that killed him, not material poison, but
> mesmeric poison . . . Mesmerism will make an apple burn the
> hand so that the child will cry . . . .[25]

From that day on, she was found planning for the future of her church and now also for a college, devoting every ounce of energy to building Christian Science into a world-wide movement.

THE CHURCH GROWS

While en route on her return to Boston, she telegraphed Calvin A. Frye, a young machinist of Lawrence, Massachusetts, who had studied with her, and asked him to meet her at Plymouth, New Hampshire.

This meeting was to change the whole course of his life. For from that time on, Calvin Frye never left Mrs. Eddy for a single day, until

---

[25]Mesmerism - Hypnosis as induced by F.A. Mesmer; hypnotism.

she passed away twenty-eight years later. Such a devotion undoubtedly played a major part in making it possible for Mary Baker Eddy to make such great strides in the growth of Christian Science.

Mary Baker Eddy at this time was sixty-two. How many men or women at age sixty-two would start out on a venture that would encompass a world-wide program. When one reflects on this they can see the boundless energy and determination that was to be Mary Baker Eddy's.

In the summer of 1876, prior to Asa Eddy's death, the Christian Scientist Association was formed. This was the second attempt at organization. It differed from the first attempt in that it made no direct effort to enlist the interest of the general public. Rather than a missionary outreach, its purpose was solely devotional.

In fact, from 1866 to her publication of the first edition of *Science and Health* in 1875, Mary Baker Eddy was convinced that church organization was a hindrance rather than a help.

She wrote in *Science and Health* in the first edition (pages 166-167):

> We have no need of creeds and church organizations to sustain or explain a demonstrable platform that defines itself in healing the sick, casting out error . . . . The mistake the disciples of Jesus made to found religious organizations and church rites, if indeed they did this, was one the Master did not make . . . No time was lost by our Master in organizations, rites, and ceremonies, or in proselytizing for certain forms of belief.

However, on August 23, 1879, a charter was issued to Mrs. Eddy, and she and some of her students met together, elected officers, and chose a name,

"The Church of Christ (Scientist)."

After her meeting with Calvin Frye in August of 1882, she reopened her metaphysical college and moved its headquarters to a new location—571 Columbus Avenue, Boston.

In 1883, she founded the *Journal of Christian Science*. Afterwards it became known as *The Christian Science Journal*. The first issue appeared on April 14, 1883.

Both in the pulpit and to her students, Mrs. Eddy often came out with unusual explanations to questions. A woman in the audience of one meeting asked Mrs. Eddy if she thought it was Christian for Mrs. Eddy "to wear purple velvet and diamonds?"

COMPARATIVE CHARTS

on

The Source of Authority
The Deity and Doctrine of Christ
The Doctrine of Salvation
The Existence of Sickness and Death
The Doctrine of The Last Things

THE BIBLE

vs.

CHRISTIAN SCIENCE

Published by SALEM KIRBAN Inc., Kent Road, Huntingdon Valley, Penna. 19006. Copyright © 1974 by Salem Kirban. Printed in the United States of America. All rights reserved, including the right to reproduce this book or portions thereof in any form.
Library of Congress Catalog Card No. 75-124142

The Source of Authority

Christian Science

Their writings show that to them the Bible is NOT the sole source of authority! "In the latter half of the nineteenth century I discovered the Science of Christianity. In 1895 I ordained that the Bible, and *Science and Health with Key to the Scriptures,* the Christian Science textbook, be the pastor, on this planet, of all the churches of the Christian Science denomination. Whenever and wherever a church of Christian Science is established, its pastor is the Bible and my book." Mary Baker Eddy, *Miscellaneous Writings* (Boston: The Christian Science Publishing Society, 1896), pp. 382, 383.

"A student—in the tongue of the world called a patient—who says to the Scientist, 'I take so much comfort in reading my Bible,' if guided wisely, will be answered, 'Let your Bible alone for three months or more. Don't open it even, or think of it, but dig night and day at *Science and Health'.*" *Christian Science Journal,* October, 1890.

"No human pen nor tongue taught me the Science contained in this book, *Science and Health . . .*" (p. 110)

"A Christian Scientist requires my work *Science and Health* for his textbook . . . because it is the voice of Truth to this age . . . Hence it gave the first rules for demonstrating this Science, and registered the revealed Truth uncontaminated by human hypotheses . . ." (pp. 456, 457)

"Christian Science is unerring and Divine . . ." (p. 99)

The weekly sermon in all Christian Science churches consists of extracts from the Bible, and from *Science and Health,* read to the congregation. The First Reader reads from *Science and Health.* Then, the Second Reader reads those passages from the Bible.

The Text

"The decisions by vote of Church Councils as to what should and should not be considered Holy Writ; the manifest mistakes in the ancient versions; the thirty thousand different readings in the Old Testament, and the three hundred thousand in the New—these facts show how a mortal and material sense stole into the divine record, with its own hue darkening to some extent the inspired pages." (p. 139)

Is the Adam and Eve Account in Error?

"Did the divine and infinite Principle become a finite deity, that He should now be called Jehovah? With a single command, Mind had made man, both male and female. How then could a material organization become the basis of man? How could the non-intelligent become the medium of Mind, and error be the enunciator of Truth? Matter is not the reflection of Spirit, yet God is reflected in all His creation. Is this addition to His creation [Genesis 2:7] real or unreal? Is it the truth, or is it a lie concerning man and God? It must be a lie, for God presently curses the ground." (p. 524)

"The literal rendering of the Scriptures makes them nothing valuable, but often is the foundation of unbelief and hopelessness. The metaphysical rendering is health and peace and hope for all." Mary Baker Eddy, *Miscellaneous Writings* (Boston: The Christian Science Publishing Society, 1896), p. 169.

Page numbers refer to *Science and Health with Key to the Scriptures,* unless another title is named.

The Bible

Mrs. Eddy is anxious to establish the point that she is the sole inventor of her new faith and teaching. In this admission she condemns herself as another in that long list of false prophets who run to teach their own thoughts without ever having been sent from God.

I have not sent these prophets, yet they ran; I have not spoken to them, yet they prophesied.

But if they had stood in my counsel, and had caused my people to hear my words, then they should have turned them from their evil way, and from the evil of their doings.

Am I a God at hand, saith the Lord, and not a God afar off? Can any hide himself in secret places that I shall not see him? saith the Lord. Do not I fill heaven and earth? saith the Lord.

I have heard what the prophets said, who prophesy lies in my name, saying, I have dreamed, I have dreamed.

How long shall this be in the heart of the prophets that prophesy lies? Yea, they are prophets of the deceit of their own heart. (Jeremiah 23:21-26)

The Text

Jesus Christ Himself accepted the Old Testament as God's Word and He vouched for the New Testament which was to come—inspired by the Spirit of God.

Then He said unto them, O foolish ones, and slow of heart to believe all that the prophets have spoken!

Ought not Christ to have suffered these things, and to enter into His glory?

And beginning at Moses, and all the prophets, He expounded unto them, in all the Scriptures, the things concerning Himself. (Luke 24:25-27)

All Scripture is given by inspiration of God, and is profitable for doctrine, for reproof, for correction, for instruction in righteousness. (2 Timothy 3:16)

But the Comforter, who is the Holy Spirit, whom the Father will send in my name, He shall teach you all things, and bring all things to your remembrance, whatever I have said unto you. (John 14:26)

I have yet many things to say unto you, but ye can not bear them now.

Nevertheless, when He, the Spirit of truth is come, He will guide you into all truth; for He shall not speak of Himself, but whatever He shall hear, that shall He speak; and He will show you things to come. (John 16:12-13)

Mrs. Eddy, fortunately or unfortunately, knows little of the subject of textual criticism and her words reflect gross misunderstandings concerning the state and the preservation by God of the texts of Holy Writ —Gary G. Cohen, Th.D.

Is the Adam and Eve Account in Error?

Jesus Christ, in Matthew 19:4 shows His absolute faith in the truth of the Adam and Eve account. Mrs. Eddy questions the wisdom of it!

The Pharisees also came unto Him, testing Him and saying unto Him, Is it lawful for a man to put away his wife for every cause?

And He answered and said unto them, Have ye not read that He who made them at the beginning made them male and female; And said, For this cause shall a man leave father and mother, and shall cleave to his wife, and they two shall be one flesh? (Matthew 19:3-5)

The Existence of Sickness and Death

Christian Science

"Sickness, disease, and death proceed from fear." (p. 260)

". . . it is impossible for matter to suffer, to feel pain or heat, to be thirsty or sick. Destroy fear, and you end fever . . . (p. 376)

The cause of all so-called disease is mental . . ." (p. 377)

"Man is never sick, for Mind is not sick and matter cannot be." (p. 393)

"Any material evidence of death is false, for it contradicts the spiritual facts of being." (p. 584)

"In reality man never dies. The belief that he dies will not establish his scientific harmony. Death is not the result of Truth but of error, and one error will not correct another." (p. 486)

"Life is real, and death is the illusion." (p. 428)

"Matter and death are mortal illusions." (p. 289)

Page numbers refer to *Science and Health with Key to the Scriptures.*

Phineas Parkhurst Quimby

The Bible

The Bible clearly affirms the real existence of matter, sickness, and death. Christian Science's denial of these is a denial of reality, and hence a falsehood in pious garb.

Behold My hands and My feet, that it is I myself; handle Me, and see; for a spirit hath not flesh and bones, as ye see Me have. (Luke 24:39)

And His disciples asked Him, saying, Master, who did sin, this man, or his parents, that he was born blind?

Jesus answered, Neither hath this man sinned, nor his parents, but that the works of God should be made manifest in him.

When he had thus spoken, He spat on the ground, and made clay of the spittle, and annointed the eyes of the blind man with the clay,

And said unto him, Go, wash in the pool of Siloam (which is by interpretation, Sent). He went his way, therefore, and washed, and came seeing. (John 9:2,3,6,7)

Yet I thought it necessary to send to you Epaphroditus . . . For, indeed, he was sick near unto death, but God had mercy on him; and not on him only, but on me also, lest I should have sorrow upon sorrow. (Philippians 2:25,27)

Then said Jesus unto them plainly, Lazarus is dead. (John 11:14)

Nov. 1859 **VI**

Is disease a belief? I say, it is, for an insane man is to himself just what he thinks he is & he is in his belief, sick. If I believe I am sick, I am sick, for my feelings are my sickness & my sickness is my belief & my belief is my mind. therefore all disease is in the mind or belief. Now as our belief or disease is made up of ideas which are matter: it is necessary to know what we are in, for, to cure the disease is to correct the error, & as disease is what follows

Above is from original manuscript written by P. P. Quimby two years *before* Mary Baker Eddy first visited Dr. Quimby and seven years *before* Mrs. Eddy claimed she discovered the "Science of Metaphysical Healing."

The Doctrine of The Last Things

	Christian Science	The Bible
The Hereafter	"The sin and error which possess us at the instant of death do not cease at that moment, but endure until the death of these errors." (p. 290) "Universal salvation rests on progression and probation, and is unattainable without them. Heaven is not a locality, but a divine state of Mind...." "No final judgment awaits mortals, for the judgment-day of wisdom comes hourly and continually, even the judgment by which mortal man is divested of all material error." (p. 291) "Man's probation after death is the necessity of his immortality; for good dies not and evil is self-destructive, therefore evil must be mortal and self-destroyed. If man should not progress after death, but should remain in error, he would be inevitably self-annihilated." (*Misc. Writings*, p. 2)	As with the Jehovah's Witnesses, Christian Science falsely claims that those who "remain in error" after death ... and do not perfect themselves in this purgatory or probation period ... will be annihilated. Mrs. Eddy's statement that "No final judgment awaits mortals," is in open opposition to the clear Biblical teaching on this subject. When the Son of man shall come in His glory, and all the holy angels with Him, then shall He sit upon the throne of His glory. And before Him shall be gathered all the nations; and He shall separate them one from another, as a shepherd divideth his sheep from the goats. And He shall set the sheep on His right hand, but the goats on the left. And these shall go away into everlasting punishment, but the righteous into life eternal. (Matthew 25:31-33,46)
Hell	"I am asked, 'Is there a hell?' Yes, there is a hell for all who persist in breaking the Golden Rule or in disobeying the commandments of God. Physical science has sometimes argued that the internal fires of our earth will eventually consume this planet. Christian Science shows that hidden unpunished sin is this internal fire — even the fire of a guilty conscience, waking to a true sense of itself, and burning in torture until the sinner is consumed — his sins destroyed.... The advanced psychist knows that his hell is mental, and that the Christian has no part in it." (*Miscellany*, p. 160) "The olden opinion that hell is fire and brimstone, has yielded somewhat to the metaphysical fact that suffering is a thing of mortal mind instead of body: so, in place of material flames and odor, mental anguish is generally accepted as the penalty for sin." (*Misc. Writings*, p. 237)	The Bible teaches that hell is not merely "mental anguish;" it is a real place wherein all the unrepentent sinners will be cast, forever separated from God. In Revelation 20:6 it is called the "Second Death." And then will I profess unto them, I never knew you; depart from me, ye that work iniquity. (Matthew 7:21-23) And the devil that deceived them was cast into the lake of fire and brimstone, where the beast and the false prophet are, and shall be tormented day and night forever and ever. And whosoever was not found written in the book of life was cast into the lake of fire. (Revelation 20:10,15)
Heaven	"Heaven is not a locality, but a divine state of Mind in which all the manifestations of Mind are harmonious and immortal, because sin is not there ..." (p. 291) "Heaven is spiritual." (*Miscellany*, p. 267) "The dying or the departed enter heaven in proportion to their progress, in proportion to their fitness to partake of the quality and the quantity of heaven ... Heaven is the reign of Divine Science. (*Miscellany*, p. 267)	Heaven, according to the Bible, is not merely a happy "state of Mind." It is an actual reality and the Dead in Christ are there today, in the true manifest presence of Christ. In My Father's house are many mansions; if it were not so, I would have told you. I go to prepare a place for you. (John 14:2) We are confident, I say, and willing rather to be absent from the body, and to be present with the Lord. (2 Corinthians 5:8) And I saw a new heaven and a new earth: for the first heaven and the first earth were passed away, and there was no more sea. And I, John, saw the holy city, new Jerusalem, coming down from God out of heaven prepared as a bride adorned for her husband. (Revelation 21:1-2)

blasphemous. Jesus' return will be an actual reality—and He will return in the same body in which He was crucified.

And while they looked steadfastly toward heaven as He went up, behold, two men stood by them in white apparel;
Who also said, Ye men of Galilee, why stand ye gazing up into heaven? This same Jesus, who is taken up from you into heaven, shall so come in like manner as ye have seen him go into heaven. (Act 1:10-11)
For the Lord Himself shall descend from heaven with a shout, with the voice of the archangel, and with the trump of God; and the dead in Christ shall rise first;
Then we who are alive and remain shall be caught up together with them in the clouds to meet the Lord in the air; and so shall we ever be with the Lord. (1 Thessalonians 4:16-17)

to the material earth or antipode of heaven. It is a marked coincidence that those dates were the first two years of my discovery of Christian Science." (Miscellany, p. 181) [antipode: direct or exact opposite]

"According to popular belief, the 'second coming' is generally interpreted as the reappearance of Jesus on earth, and Mrs. Eddy is the first person in history to controvert this theory.

She has shown conclusively that the 'second coming' refers not to the reappearance of the human Jesus, but to the discovery of the Christ, 'The divine manifestation of God, which comes to the flesh to destroy incarnate error.'

Christ, Truth, is the Holy Ghost or divine Comforter which Jesus said would come.

Jesus manifested the 'first coming' of the Christ to mankind, and Mary Baker Eddy's discovery of Christian Science (the Comforter) has completely fulfilled the Biblical prophecy of the 'second coming.'"

Irving C. Tomlinson, Twelve Years with Mary Baker Eddy, (Boston: The Christian Science Publishing Society, 1945), p. 13.

The Resurrection of the Body

NO RESURRECTION OF THE BODY
"Resurrection. Spiritualization of thought a new and higher idea of immortality, or spiritual existence; material belief yielding to spiritual understanding." (p 53)

"No resurrection from the grave awaits Mind or Life, for the grave has no power over either." (p. 291)

Christian Scientists deny Christ's resurrection from the dead. (p. 291)

The Bible over and over declares that Christ rose bodily from the grave. Jesus saith unto them, Come and dine. And none of the disciples dared ask Him, Who art thou? knowing that it was the Lord. Jesus then cometh, and taketh bread, and giveth them, and fish likewise.
This is now the third time that Jesus showed Himself to His disciples, after He was risen from the dead. (John 21:12-14)
And He said unto them, Why are ye troubled? And why do thoughts arise in your hearts? Behold my hands and my feet, that it is I myself; handle Me and see; for a spirit hath not flesh and bones, as ye see Me have. And when He had thus spoken, He showed them His hands and His feet. (Luke 24:33-40)

The Final Judgment

NO FINAL JUDGMENT
"No final judgment awaits mortals, for the judgment-day of wisdom comes hourly and continually, even the judgment by which mortal man is divested of all material error." (p. 291)

A final judgment does indeed await every mortal.
And I saw the dead, small and great stand before God, and the books were opened; and another book was opened, which is the book of life. And the dead were judged out of those things which were written in the books, according to their works. (Revelation 20:12)

The New Heavens and New Earth

NO NEW HEAVENS NOR NEW EARTH
"This sacred city, described in the Apocalypse (21:16) ... represents the light and glory of divine Science. The builder and maker of this New Jerusalem is God ... and it is 'a city which hath foundations.' The description is metaphoric. Spiritual teaching must always be by symbols..."

"Taken in its allegorical sense, the description of the city as foursquare has profound meaning. The four sides of our city are the Word, Christ, Christianity, and divine Science." (p. 575)

The Bible declares that this present earth and its atmosphere will be consumed with fire, and that the Creator will make new ones upon which the redeemed will dwell forever.
But the day of the Lord will come as a thief in the night; in the which the heavens shall pass away with a great noise and the elements shall also melt with fervent heat, the earth also and the works that are therein shall be burned up ...
Nevertheless we, according to His promise, look for new heavens and a new earth, wherein dwelleth righteousness. (2 Peter 3:10,13)

Major George W. Glover
Mrs. Eddy's first husband

Daniel Patterson
Mrs. Eddy's second husband

Asa Gilbert Eddy
Mrs. Eddy's third husband

Mark Baker
Mrs. Eddy's father

Ebenezer J. Foster Eddy
Adopted son of Mrs. Eddy

George Washington Glover
Mrs. Eddy's only child

Mrs. Eddy replied,

> There are ladies here, I presume, with much more expensive dresses on. This purple velvet is 'purple' but it is velveteen that I paid $1.50 for, and I have worn it for several years, but it seems to be perpetually renewed like the widow's cruse.

> The cross and ring were given me by those who have been healed in Christian Science, with the request that I wear them.[26]

Georgine Milmine in her book, *The Life of Mary Baker G. Eddy,* states:

> When she lectured before her classes, Mrs. Eddy usually had a vase of flowers upon a table at her side, and, to illustrate the non-existence of matter, she often explained that there were really no flowers there at all, and that the bouquet was merely a belief of mortal mind. She was fond of flowers, in spite of the fact that she had always been totally without a sense of smell— she used, indeed, to tell her students that the absence of physical sense meant a gain in spirituality.[27]

Mrs. Eddy also taught that the natural law which produces flowers and fruit can be changed at will. In a personal letter written in 1896 she stated that she had caused an apple tree to blossom in January, and frequently "some such trifles in the floral line," while living in Lynn, Massachusetts.[28]

More than once someone would stand to ask her, in accusing tones, why she , Mary Baker Eddy, this exponent of mind over matter, occasionally wore glasses during her platform experiences.

There is no record that she came up with a plausible answer. In fact, the use of glasses off and on through the years has proved to be a stumbling block to many of her followers. Mrs. Eddy even had teeth extracted under local anaesthesia. On page 464 of *Science and Health* she wrote:

> If from an injury or from any cause, a Christian Scientist were seized with pain so violent that he could not treat himself mentally,—and the Scientists had failed to relieve him,—the sufferer could call a surgeon, who would give him a

---

[26]Kennedy, *Mrs. Eddy . . . .,* p. 298.
[27]Milmine, *The Life of Mary Baker G. Eddy,* p. 300.
[28]*Ibid.,* p. 186.

hypodermic injection, then, when the belief of pain was lulled, he could handle his own case mentally.[29]

By 1884 there were sixty-one persons that belonged to the Christian Scientists' Association, but her fame was spreading world-wide and soon this new religion would grow very rapidly. By this time, Mrs. Eddy was now president of the Massachusetts Metaphysical College, editor of the *Christian Science Journal,* president of the Christian Scientists' Association, and pastor of the First Church of Christ (Scientist). Her classes averaged 25 students and the course of instruction which she gave was three weeks. Adding this up, it would mean that Mrs. Eddy's fees for each three week period would amount to $7500.

With the growth of *The Journal of Christian Science,* copies were finding their way not only all over the United States, but also throughout the world.

And each Christmas, the gifts that individuals gave to Mrs. Eddy at this season were printed in the *Journal.*

As an example in 1889, she received such Christmas gifts as: an eider-down pillow, white satin with gold embroidery; a pastel painting of Minnehaha Falls; perfumery; Bible Pearls of Promise; and two fat Kentucky turkeys.

The *Journal* had a popular column called "The Healing Department." In this department many people recited the details of their illnesses, and how they were healed. One of them, curiously enough, was headlined,

"Cured of Both Paralysis and Mormonism."

In the first issue of *The Journal,* April 1883, there were fourteen authorized healers listed in its columns. By April 1885, it had grown to forty-three, and by 1887, there were one hundred and ten Christian Science practitioners, plus nineteen Christian Science Institutes and Academies.

For most, a degree from the Massachusetts Metaphysical College meant a lucrative practice.

In August 1885, Mrs. Eddy became acquainted with Rev. James Henry Wiggin. Mr. Wiggin was a Unitarian minister. He soon became Mrs. Eddy's literary advisor. She brought him her book, *Science and Health,* which she had just corrected from the fourth edition, 1884.

---

[29]Mary Baker Eddy, *Science and Health . . . ,* p. 464.

Mr. Wiggin, upon seeing the manuscript, told Mrs. Eddy that it needed to be rewritten and not simply corrected. She consented to his doing this. The 1875 edition, up to the 1886 edition, were each rewritten by Mr. Wiggin, putting into more readable English, the ideas which Mrs. Eddy had arranged somewhat haphazardly.

A typical example is a statement taken from her chapter on the Atonement, in 1884:

Mrs. Eddy wrote:

> The glorious spiritual signification of the life and not death of our Master—for he never died—was laying down all of earth to instruct his enemies the way to Heaven, showing in the most sublime and unequivocal sense how Heaven is obtained.

Mr. Wiggin's revision was:

> The material blood of Jesus was no more efficacious to cleanse from sin, when it was shed upon 'the accursed tree,' than when it was flowing in his veins as he went daily about his Father's business.[30]

Finally, becoming annoyed with Mr. Wiggin's corrections, in 1890, she severed connections with him.

In a letter to an old college friend, dated December 14, 1889, Mr. Wiggin wrote as follows:

> Christian Science, on its theological side, is an ignorant revival of one form of ancient gnosticism, that Jesus is to be distinguished from the Christ, and that His earthly appearance was phantasmal, not real and fleshly . . . .
>
> Religiously, Christian Science is a revolt from orthodoxy, but unphilosophically conducted, endeavouring to ride two horses . . . .
>
> As for clearness, many Christian Science people thought her earlier editions [before Wiggin] much better, because they sounded more *like* Mrs. Eddy. The truth is, she does not care to have her paragraphs clear, and delights in so expressing herself that her words may have various readings and meanings. Really, that is one of the tricks of the trade.[31]

With her Metaphysical College growing, she decided not only to have her "primary course," which was the twelve lesson initial class which cost $300, but she also decided to institute other additional courses.

---

[30]*Ibid.*, p. 25.

[31]Milmine, *The Life of Mary Baker G. Eddy*, pp. 337, 338.

NORMAL CLASS NOTES

PREPARED AND USED BY

Edward A. Kimball, C.S.D.

TO TEACH THE

FIRST NORMAL CLASS TAUGHT

IN THE

Board of Education

OF

Mary Baker Eddy's

MASSACHUSETTS METAPHYSICAL COLLEGE

The universe is spiritual because all cause is Spirit, Mind. The flower, bird, landscape, rock, house, stomach, eye, hand, arm, leg, head, all are spiritual. Mortals, placing substance, cause, law as matter and material, of necessity view things from a material point of view. And this is all that ever makes them seem sick and dying. When mortals change their viewpoint, we will have flowers that cannot fade, birds, animals, men that cannot sicken and die, and stomachs that cannot be disturbed, legs that cannot be lame, eyes that cannot be blind, as matter.

Cause. There is no cause for *abnormal growths.* God's activity as creative Principle is the only cause. There can be no abnormal growth anywhere for cause, God, has made all that was made, and it never made inaction or matter. Therefore, this so-called tumor is not tumor, or matter, but belief, subjectively and self-imposed.

What heals the sick? There never was a sick man or a sick woman. There is no sickness to be healed. Christian Science never healed sickness. Why? First, because there is no sickness to be healed. Second, because the infinite Principle knows no such thing. There is no such thing as mortal mind belief or manifestation of belief. There is no sick body. No one has measles. No measles.

Christian Science Lesson Plan as taught by Edward A. Kimball.

They included a course in Metaphysical Obstetrics, and a course in Theology, as well as, what she termed a "Normal course"—this being a review of the Primary course.

Below will give you an idea of the tuition fees which she, the sole instructor, received for each of these courses:

Primary Class, twelve lessons $300
    (afterward seven lessons)
Normal Class, six lessons 200
Class in Metaphysical Obstetrics 100
    (six lessons)
Class in Theology, six lessons 200
Total (if one took all 4 courses) $800

THE SANCTITY OF CHRISTIAN SCIENCE LITERATURE

During Christmas of 1887, Mrs. Eddy moved from Columbus Avenue to a more fashionable house on Commonwealth Avenue. This was announced in *The Christian Science Journal,* which in its article stated that,

> Commonwealth Avenue is the most fashionable in the city . . . .
> To name the dwellers on this Avenue would be to name scores of Boston's wealthy and influential men . . . .

Both the *Christian Science Journal* writers and Mrs. Eddy's own writings were intent on showing that Mary Baker Eddy was God's answer for today. This was exemplified by a November 1885 paragraph in the *Christian Science Journal:*

> What a triumphant career is this for a woman! Can it be anything less than the 'tabernacle of God with men'—the fulfillment of the vision of the lonely seer on the Isle of Patmos—the 'wonder in heaven,' delivering the child which shall rule all nations? How dare we say to the contrary, that she is God-sent to the world, as much as any character of Sacred Writ?

In a message by the Rev. George B. Day in a sermon delivered at the Chicago Christian Science Church, and afterward approvingly printed in the *Journal,* he declared that "Christian Science is the Gospel according to Woman." He then continued:

> We are witnessing the transfer of the gospel from male to female trust . . . . Eighteen hundred years ago Paul declared that man was head of the woman; but now, in *Science and Health,* it is asserted that 'woman is the highest form of man.'

During these periods of her life, there were several splits within her church, with members leaving because of disagreements. Partly because of this she decided to engage the services of Ebenezer J.

Foster. Foster had a degree of Doctor of Medicine, and was a graduate of Hahnemann Medical College of Philadelphia. At the time when he first met Mary Baker Eddy, he was about forty, and was practicing in Waterbury, Vermont. He became a student in Mrs. Eddy's classes, and Mary Baker Eddy, faced with a bitter crisis in her movement, felt she needed someone in whom she could place her confidence.

So, on November 5, 1888, she adopted Ebenezer Foster as her own son, and he assumed the name of Ebenezer Foster-Eddy. Dr. Foster was to teach in the now longer course of Metaphysical Obstetrics, and the tuition fee for this course was doubled to $200.

With dissension growing in her ranks, Mrs. Eddy was determined that Christian Scientists should be held even more rigidly than before to the rule forbidding them to read any but Mrs. Eddy's writings in mental healing. In fact, she even admonished beginning students to lay aside the Bible in favor of *Science and Health*. The *Journal* also instructed Mrs. Eddy's students to burn all forbidden literature.

> Burn every scrap of 'Christian Science literature,' so-called, except *Science and Health* and the publications bearing the imprint of the Christian Science Publishing Society of Boston.

The *Journal* in October, 1890, also stated,

> A student—in the tongue of the world called a patient—who says to the Scientist, 'I take so much comfort in reading my Bible,' if guided wisely, will be answered, 'Let your Bible alone for three months or more. Don't open it even, or think of it, but dig night and day at *Science and Health*.'

This statement caused quite an uproar among many dissenting Christian Scientists, and the Publication Committee later retracted these sentiments.

By April 1890, there were at least 250 healers and 33 Academies and Institutes teaching Christian Science. In those days, the healer's usual charge was $1 a treatment, or daily treatments at $5 a week.

By 1890, the dissension in her Boston church became so great that she decided to dissolve the church. On May 21, 1894, the cornerstone of the now existing Mother Church was laid on a lot purchased on Falmouth Street in Boston. This time, Mrs. Eddy was in control of the new Boston church because it was an institution without congregational government. It was to be controlled by four directors whom she would appoint. Its directors were pledged to see that the church taught only what was in the seventy-first edition of *Science*

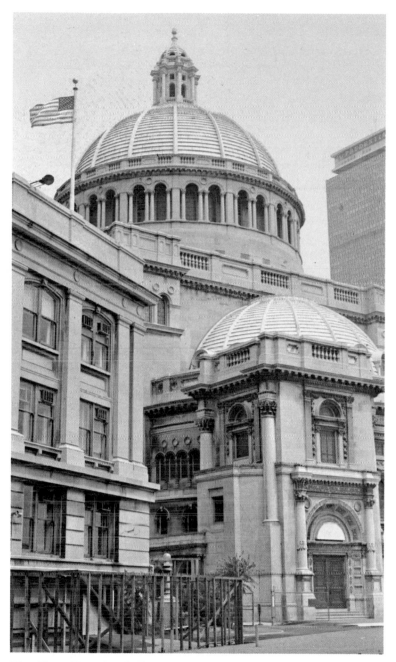

The First Church of Christ, Scientist, in Boston, Massachusetts.
Referred to by its members as The Mother Church.

and Health and whatever Mrs. Eddy might put in subsequent editions. Perhaps the fourth point was most important. If the directors did not comply with her instructions, they were bound to give back the ground and building to Mrs. Eddy and to her heirs forever.

The Mother Church was dedicated on January 6, 1895. There were so many people there that it was necessary to repeat the service four times. It had a membership of almost 3,000 people, but Mrs. Eddy did not attend, perhaps because of her failing strength.

MRS. WOODBURY'S "PRINCE OF PEACE"

Mrs. Eddy had many experiences of former students who had become leaders in the Christian Science Church, who would be a cause of embarrassment to her.

One of these was Josephine Woodbury. Josephine Woodbury was a very active individual who made lecture tours as far west as Denver. She frequently wrote for the *Journal*, and became a qualified teacher.

She had such an outgoing personality that it was difficult for Mary Baker Eddy to keep Mrs. Woodbury in line. Apparently, Josephine Woodbury believed in the unconventional, for in the summer of 1890 she announced to her friends and students that she was about to give birth to a child which had been immaculately conceived. Naturally this announcement became a front-page story. Mrs. Eddy, struggling with many other problems was soon confronted with another problem which bordered on the ridiculous.

She tried to make Mrs. Woodbury revise her thinking. Mrs. Woodbury not only refused to change her stand, but, when the child was born she named him, "The Prince of Peace." She even went on further to declare that Mrs. Eddy herself had fortold the event.

In 1896, Josephine Woodbury was "forever excommunicated" from the Church.

THE MONEY ROLLS IN

Mary Baker Eddy was very successful in building her Mother Church. She was concerned that the work would go forward rapidly, so she asked forty of her students to contribute $1,000 each immediately. The new church was dedicated January 6, 1895. The final cost of the building was over $250,000. There were more than 6,000 people who attended the dedicatory exercises.

In 1889, Mrs. Eddy decided it was time for her to retire to Concord, New Hampshire. Even in her retirement, she was still busy writing

Pleasant View, Concord, New Hampshire, where Mary Baker Eddy lived for 16 years.

49

and rewriting *Science and Health*—as she had been doing for twenty years prior.

As an example, new editions of the book came out in 1891, 1894, and 1896. Loyal Christian Scientists were expected to purchase **each** new edition at $3.18 a volume.

In her book, *Miscellaneous Writings,* first published in 1897, she stated in part,

> The Bible, *Science and Health With Key to the Scriptures,* and my other published works are the only proper instructors for this hour. It shall be the duty of all Christian Scientists to circulate and to sell as many of these books as they can. If a member of the First Church of Christ Scientist shall fail to obey this injunction, it shall render him liable to lose his membership in this church.[32]

The 1891 edition of *Science and Health* alone sold over 150,000 copies. In 1893, she received $12,000 in royalties, in 1894, $15,000, and in 1895, $18,000.

In those days, prior to inflation, these were extremely large amounts of money.

Another on whom she was to rely so much, Ebenezer J. Foster-Eddy, her adopted son, was to prove a sore disappointment to her. With disturbing stories reaching her about his personal conduct and rumors of his improprieties with a married woman in his office, it finally became necessary for her in the spring of 1896 to take the publishing business away from her son, and transfer it to Joseph Armstrong, a Christian Scientist who had formally been a banker in Kansas.

MRS. EDDY RETIRES

Mrs. Eddy continued to withdraw from public contact and to seclude herself at Pleasant View.

In fact, it was a full three months after the completion of the Mother Church in Boston before she first saw it . . . and it was another two months after that until she even occupied its pulpit for the first time on Sunday, May 26, 1895. She was to only make one more appearance there, in February 1896.

The Church now had a general membership of 1,500 people. The Church membership was growing so fast that many of Mrs. Eddy's followers had never seen their leader.

---

[32]*Christian Science Journal,* March, 1897.

She invited the congregation to call upon her at Pleasant View in Concord, New Hampshire, after the Church's annual communion. (The communion is observed once a year on the second Sunday in June. No "material" emblems such as bread and wine are offered, and the communion is one of silent thought.)

One hundred and eighty Christian Scientists arrived at Pleasant View, and Mrs. Eddy shook hands with each delegate personally.

In 1897, 2,500 pilgrims made this annual pilgrimage. By 1901, 3,000 came up to Concord. This time they were not admitted to the house at Pleasant View, but Mrs. Eddy appeared briefly at the balcony.

The last pilgrimage occurred in 1904. This time the pilgrims met in the New Christian Science Church in Concord, New Hampshire. Fifteen hundred of them gathered there. Mrs. Eddy's carriage approached the church, and there from her carriage she spoke her greeting to the president of the Mother Church. This was her last official appearance.

In 1895, Mary Baker Eddy had adopted the title, "Mother." By 1903, however, partially because of a ridiculing article written by Mark Twain, this title was dropped, and it was suggested that she be called, "Leader."

In his later years, Mark Twain regretted some of his caustic comments on Christian Science and wrote, concerning Mary Baker Eddy:

> She launched a world-religion which is increasing at the rate of a new church every four days. I believe that the new religion will conquer half of Christendom in a hundred years . . . .[33]

After the pilgrimages were discontinued, there was really no way that her devoted followers could ever see Mrs. Eddy. Many used to go to Concord, and stand by the road where they knew that Mrs. Eddy's carriage would pass. This became a source of annoyance to her, and in a new bylaw in the church manual, she rebuked them with the following:

> *Thou Shalt not Steal.* Sect. 15. Neither a Christian Scientist, his student or his patient, nor a member of the Mother Church shall daily and continuously haunt Mrs. Eddy's drive by meeting her once or more every day when she goes out—on penalty of being disciplined and dealt with justly by her church . . . .[34]

---

[33]Kennedy, *Mrs. Eddy . . .*, p. 431.

[34]Milmine, *The Life of Mary Baker G. Eddy*, p. 445.

Mrs. Eddy was so singularly dedicated to her work, that this perhaps was the basic reason for the neglect of her only son. After George Washington Glover went West with the Cheney's in 1857, he did not see his mother again until 1879. His longest stay in Boston was in 1888 when he brought his family to meet his mother. While his relations with his mother were friendly, they were usually of a very formal nature. In fact, Mrs. Eddy had written him that she had no room for him in her house and forbade him even to come as evidenced by a letter written from Boston, October 31, 1887, which in part reads:

> Dear George:
>
> Yours received. I'm surprised that you think of coming to visit me when I live in a schoolhouse and have no room that I can let even a boarder into . . . . Besides this, I have all I can meet without receiving company. I must have quiet in my house . . . . Boston is the last place in the world for you or your family. When I retire from business and into private life, then I can receive you if you are reformed, but not otherwise.[35]

On January 2 of 1907, Mr. Glover and his daughter, Mary Baker Glover, were given a brief interview with Mary Baker Eddy at Pleasant View. [In his latter years he had returned to his family name.]

A few days later, Mary Baker Eddy wrote to her son, asking him to return all the letters that she had written to him.

Her son refused to give up the letters, and in fact, brought a suit against the ten most prominent Christian Scientists, including the officers of the Mother Church in Boston, stating that Mrs. Eddy was incompetent through age and failing faculties to manage her estate. He requested that a receiver of her property be appointed and that the defendants named be required to account for alleged misuse of her property. Mrs. Eddy, however, met this action a few days later by declaring a trusteeship for the control of her estate. By August of that year, Mr. Glover withdrew his suit.

The lawsuit disclosed an interesting fact. In 1907 she had approximately $1,000,000.00 worth of taxable property!

RETURN TO BOSTON

On Sunday, January 26, 1908, Mrs. Eddy left Pleasant View at Concord, New Hampshire, and boarded a special train which was to take her to her final residence in Boston, Massachusetts. This residence was a mansion in Newton, a suburb of Boston.

---

[35]*Ibid.*, pp. 454-55.

Mary Baker Eddy's last residence at Chestnut Hill, a mansion in Newton...a suburb of Boston.

53

She had a new Victrola, and she often joined her household in accompanying its records, singing the old favorite songs of those days, such as, "Comin' Through the Rye," "The Old Oaken Bucket," and "Home, Sweet Home."

It was a cold frosty day on the first of December, 1910, when Mrs. Eddy took her usual drive around the roads of Chestnut Hill, in her carriage.

This was to be her last trip.

On December 3, 1910, Mrs. Eddy died at 89 years of age.

Mary Baker Eddy was **50** years of age before she really knew what she wanted to do. She was **60** before she discovered the most effective way of doing it, that is, by founding a church. She was **70** when she achieved her greatest triumph. This was the reorganization of her church and the taking of personal control of its Mother Church.

Mrs. Eddy had long ago realized that the biggest danger to the purity of her movement lay in the pastors of her branch churches. These pastors soon became leaders in the Christian Science movement in their home communities, and unless properly controlled, Mrs. Eddy considered this very dangerous.

In 1895, she wrote:

> In 1895 I ordained the Bible and *Science and Health with Key to the Scriptures,* as the Pastor, on this planet, of all the churches of the Christian Science Denomination.

In the *Journal* of April, 1895, she further stated that there were to be no more preachers . . . that each church should have instead a First and a Second Reader. The Sunday sermon was to consist of extracts from the Bible, and from *Science and Health, read* to the congregation. The First Reader reads from *Science and Health.* Then the Second Reader reads from passages from the Bible which Mrs. Eddy had selected. In a notice to the churches in 1897, Mrs. Eddy said, in effect, that this was "authorized by Christ."

Readers were forbidden to read from a manuscript or from a transcribed copy. They were told that they must read from *Science and Health* itself, and that they should at no time make any remarks explanatory of the passages which they read. Before beginning to read from Mrs. Eddy's book, the instructions to the reader were that, "he shall distinctly announce its full title, and give the author's name."

Mary Baker Eddy's study on second floor of Chestnut Hill home.

In his book, *Twelve Years with Mary Baker Eddy,* Irving C. Tomlinson writes:

> For centuries, theologians, Bible students, and Christians of all denominations have been in a state of eager expectancy regarding what is usually referred to as the *second coming.* According to popular belief, the *second coming* is generally interpreted as the reappearance of Jesus on earth, and Mrs. Eddy is the first person in history to controvert this theory.
>
> She has shown conclusively that the *second coming* refers not to the reappearance of the human Jesus, but to the discovery of the Christ, The divine manifestation of God, which comes to the flesh to destroy incarnate error. Christ, Truth, is the Holy Ghost or divine Comforter which Jesus said would come.
>
> Jesus manifested the 'first coming' of the Christ to mankind, and Mary Baker Eddy's discovery of Christian Science (the Comforter) has completely fulfilled the Biblical prophecy of the 'second coming.'[36]

The top executive branch of Christian Science, is today a permanent five-member Board of Directors. The chairmanship rotates among them on an annual basis.

While no one knows the exact number of Christian Scientists in the world, it is known that there are over 3,200 Christian Science Churches in fifty-eight countries. Two-thirds of them are in the United States. These statistics are current as of 1973.

The Church of Christ (Scientist) recently erected a $75 million church complex in Boston. This includes a 28-story concrete administration tower, a Sunday School building, and an international broadcasting and audio-visual center. A recent chairman of the Christian Science Board stated:

> Services are becoming less formalized. Young people don't like stiff, formal services . . . . Now we have youngsters showing up in blue jeans and sometimes even barefoot. We urge others in the congregation not to be shocked, but to take them as they come . . . .

Mary Baker Eddy in writing the church manual stated that the laws which she instituted were not subject to amendment. In Article 25, she provided that no tenet or bylaw could be amended or annulled without her written consent. Since she died in 1910, the laws of the church manual are irrevocable.

---

[36]Tomlinson, *Twelve Years with Mary Baker Eddy,* pp. 213, 214.

The Christian Science 26 story Administration Building in Boston, built at a cost of $70 million and completed in June, 1973.

Mary Baker Eddy was undoubtedly a very unusual woman whose dedication to her cause meant the forfeiting of many ordinary pleasures and desires that most people would not sacrifice.

Had she abided by the Bible orthodoxy of her father, it is quite conceivable that this boundless energy and dedication would have made her a giant in the Christian faith.

With deep respect for her accomplishments in this world as an individual . . . the writer regrets that she chose to build her house upon the sand in creating her own interpretation of what God is . . . apart from the Scriptures.

And because of this, the Church of Christ Scientist has emerged as another fast growing cult among the many which continue to confuse the peoples of the world.

And as God's Word, the Bible, tells us, ". . . from such turn away" (2 Timothy 3:5).

Mary Baker Eddy memorial and tomb in Mount Auburn Cemetery in Cambridge, Massachusetts.

PRIVATE DIRECTIONS

FOR

METAPHYSICAL HEALING

BY

MARY BAKER GLOVER EDDY

Sample Lesson from Mary Baker Eddy course with excerpts of its contents.

Science teaches us the blood cannot be impure, or filled with humors, that there are no hereditary diseases, that no bad effects follow fatigue, exposure to cold or heat, from food or drink, surgical operations etc., etc.

Truth is not material and the only reality of being is its Truth and Truth is harmonious, therefore, sickness being a discord is unreal, a belief only, and that which Science destroys. Understanding this statement will destroy the belief and when the belief is destroyed the sick are healed, thus proving disease without Principle, a thing of mortal mind a belief, and because there is no mortal mind there is no sickness.

Life is never lost; there is no death; man is eternal; and because of this he is incapable of sin, sickness, or death; the body is sensationless, man is shadow.

Inflamation is nothing more nor less than fear, and fear is the foundation in mortal mind of all disease, destroy the fear of the disease and the disease will disappear.

Disease is an image in mortal mind, if a cancer, or malformation, or whatever it may be, argue it out of belief and it disappears altogether; and this is your proof that it is mind instead of matter.

Repeat often in memory so as to make it real and understood the key-note of Science that will make your practice most successful—namely—that there is no substance; Life; Intelligence or Truth in matter that all is mind and matter is but a belief.

Permit the use of no drugs or applications of any sort if you would save the sick; to use those would prevent your success.

Mind alone is able to heal the sick, *Matter cannot do it.*

MARY BAKER EDDY
(about 1890)